Placement Test and Inventories

Grades 3-6

Senior Author

Dr. Roger C. Farr

Chancellor's Professor Emeritus of Education and
Former Director of the Center for Innovation in Assessment,
Indiana University, Bloomington

Harcourt School Publishers

www.harcourtschool.com

Printed in the United States of America

ISBN 10: 0-15-380282-0
ISBN 13: 978-0-15-380282-9

2 3 4 5 6 7 8 9 10   082   16 15 14 13 12 11 10 09

Table of Contents

. . . .

© Harcourt

Appendix: Copying Masters

• •

StoryTown Assessment Components

• •

The chart below gives a brief overview of the assessment choices that are available at grades 3–6. The titles in boldface can be found in this Teacher Guide.

Entry-Level Assessments	To plan instruction
Placement Test	• To determine the best placement for a student and to assess strengths and weaknesses
Phonemic Awareness Inventory	• To determine a student's phonemic awareness skills
Phonics Inventory	• To assess the ability to apply phonic and structural analysis skills to nonsense words
Benchmark Assessments Beginning-of-Year	• To determine a student's proficiency with selected skills *before* starting instruction
Formative Assessments	**To monitor student progress**
Phonemic Inventory	• To monitor a student's ability to apply phonic and structural analysis skills
Weekly Lesson Tests Copying Masters	• To monitor a student's comprehension of each selection, selection vocabulary, and skills taught during the week
Monitor Progress notes at "point of use" in the Teacher Edition	• To monitor selected skills and strategies as they are taught
Theme Tests	• To assess mastery of reading and language skills taught in a theme
Summative Assessments	**To assess mastery of skills taught** **To assess ability to apply skills and strategies**
Benchmark Assessments • Mid-Year • End-of-Year	• To evaluate mastery of reading and language skills taught during the year.

Overview of the
Placement Test and Inventories

. . . .

This Teacher's Guide is organized into three major sections. Each section contains information about a separate assessment component. The three assessment components are as follows:

Placement Test

The Placement Test is designed to place students in the appropriate level of the program to assure that each student experiences maximum success as he or she begins instruction. The Placement Test is a multiple-choice test consisting of two subtests—Vocabulary in Context and Reading Comprehension. The test consists of a total of 54 items. It should be administered in two sessions. The levels to administer will vary depending upon the last level of a reading program the students have completed.

Copying masters of the student test materials can be found in the Appendix.

Phonemic Awareness Inventory

The Phonemic Awareness Inventory is a series of individually administered oral tests designed to assess phonemic awareness. The Phonemic Awareness Inventory would be appropriate to use for diagnosing students who are experiencing difficulty, for monitoring the results of special instruction, or to verify placement decisions.

Copying masters of the test materials are located in the Appendix.

Phonics Inventory

The Phonics Inventory is designed to assess a student's ability to apply phonics and word structure skills. The Phonics Inventory is administered individually. The student is asked to pronounce a series of nonsense words that have been carefully constructed to assess a wide range of phonic and structural elements. By analyzing a student's responses, the teacher can determine specific strengths and weaknesses in phonic and structural analysis and use that information to plan instruction.

The Phonics Inventory would be appropriate to use for diagnosing students who are experiencing difficulty, for monitoring the results of special instruction, or to verify placement decisions.

Copying masters of the Recording Form, the Performance Profile, and the word lists are located in the Appendix.

Placement Test

· ·

Purpose

The Placement Test was designed to determine students' appropriate placement levels in the reading program. Because it is an objective test consisting of multiple-choice items, it is primarily intended for group administration. However, the Placement Test may also be administered individually, using the same procedures.

The total score for each student will determine the student's initial placement level in the program and the type of support needed. The placement level does not indicate the level of material the student can read independently. Rather, it indicates the student's instructional reading level. As with all tests, careful teacher observation of the student during reading instruction is necessary to determine whether the placement level is appropriate. However, no adjustments in placement should be made unless the teacher has observed a student for at least several reading lessons.

The Placement Test is best suited for students in grades 3 through 6. Additional resources are available for other grades.

- For Kindergarten, use the Kindergarten Assessments.
- For Grade 1, use the Grade 1 Placement Test and Inventories.
- For Grade 2, use the Grade 2 Placement Test and Inventories.

Description Of The Placement Test

The Placement Test assesses general reading ability through the use of two sub-tests: Vocabulary in Context and Reading Comprehension.

Vocabulary in Context

This subtest consists of ten items for each level of the program, beginning with Grade 2, Book 1, and extending through Grade 6. Each test item is a sentence from which one word has been deleted. Following each sentence are word options that can be used to complete the sentence. Students are to select the word that best completes the sentence.

Vocabulary in Context items were developed to match the language used in the reading selections of the various levels of the program. The correct answer for each item is a vocabulary word from the program level at which the word appears. The distractors were selected to be appropriate in difficulty for the level.

Reading Comprehension

This subtest consists of a series of authentic fiction and nonfiction reading passages. Most of the test passages have been selected from children's and young adult publications to match the themes and genre used at the various reading levels of the program. There is one reading passage for each level of the program, beginning with Grade 2, Book 1. Following each reading passage are eight multiple-choice reading comprehension questions. These questions assess literal, inferential, and critical comprehension skills. One or two questions for each passage are vocabulary items

Teacher's Manual

that require students to determine the meaning of a word on the basis of the context provided in the passage. These items are somewhat similar to the items on the Vocabulary in Context subtest except that they enable the student to apply vocabulary skills in a real reading situation and sometimes require more sophisticated distinctions between various meanings of a multiple-meaning word, based on the context of the passage.

Each reading passage is preceded by a "purpose for reading" that helps the student better focus on the passage. Research has shown that when readers read for specific purposes, their comprehension is better. Furthermore, purposes for reading provide students with some clues to the overall structure or schema of the story and allow them to make better use of background knowledge in reading.

Students take three levels of the test, depending on the last level completed in their previous reading program. Always begin students one level below the last level they completed. A more detailed explanation of which levels to administer is provided in this Teacher's Guide. A summary of the passage levels and titles can be found in Table 1.

TABLE 1

Book Levels and Titles of Placement Test Passages	
Book Level	**Title of Placement Test Passage**
2-1	"Soup or Salad?"
2-2	"In the Middle of the Night"
3-1	"Dress-Up Day"
3-2	"Tuck-in Time for Mom"
4	"Follow Your Heart"
5	"How to Unearth Earthworms"
6	"Trash in the Tides"

General Test Considerations

Before Getting Started

The following suggestions will help provide for a more valid and reliable assessment.

1. Be thoroughly familiar with the Placement Test before beginning to administer the test. Look over the Vocabulary items, read the passages you will be using, and note the types of comprehension questions that are used.

2. Study Table 2, which follows in this Teacher's Guide, to determine which levels of the test to administer to your students.

3. After determining the appropriate levels of the test for your students, make a Student Booklet for each student by reproducing a cover page ("Pupil Summary of Placement Test Results"), the appropriate sample page, and the appropriate test pages, using the copying masters found in the Appendix.

4. Attempt to seat the children so that you can easily observe them. This will help you to determine if students are on the correct page when the tests are started and to see that they mark the sample items appropriately.

5. Be sure that each student has a pencil to mark responses and has written his or her name on the front of the test booklet.

6. Have on hand a demonstration copy of a student booklet as well as the directions for administering the test found in this Teacher's Guide. The general directions to the examiner are printed in regular type. The specific directions to be read aloud to the children are printed in *italic* type.

Scheduling the Test

It is suggested that the test be administered in two different sessions. The entire test takes approximately fifty minutes, but total testing time may vary with age and grade level. The two testing sessions may be scheduled in the morning and afternoon of the same day, or on two consecutive days.

The Vocabulary in Context subtest should be administered first. This subtest can be administered in one sitting of approximately twenty minutes. Most students should be able to complete the test in this time period; however, if you find that some students need more time to complete all of the test items, allow them to keep working.

The Reading Comprehension subtest should be administered in the second session. This subtest can be administered in approximately thirty minutes. Most students should be able to complete the test in this time period; however, if you find that some students need more time to complete all of the test items, allow them to keep working.

Test Items to Be Completed

Each student will complete a total of 54 items—30 Vocabulary in Context items and 24 Reading Comprehension items. The specific items to be completed depend on the reading level of the materials that the students have just completed. In general, students will complete ten Vocabulary in Context items and one reading passage with eight comprehension items for each of the following levels:

- **Below Level:** the level below the one they just completed in their previous reading program
- **On Level:** the level they just completed in their previous reading program
- **Above Level:** the level they would have been entering in their previous reading program

Always begin students one level below the last level completed. For example, if your students have just completed Book 3-1 in their previous reading program, they will take levels 2-2, 3-1, and 3-2 of the Placement Test. Table 2 indicates the specific test levels to administer. If you are unsure of the level of the previous reading program the students have completed, you should estimate the level, and then reduce this by another level. In determining reading placement, it is better to place students in a level in which they will have success rather than taking a chance on placing them in a level that will be frustrating for them.

Teacher's Manual

TABLE 2

Levels to Administer	
Level Just Completed	**Test Passages to Administer**
Book 2-2	"Soup or Salad?" (2-1) "In the Middle of the Night" (2-2) "Dress-Up Day" (3-1)
Book 3-1	"In the Middle of the Night" (2-2) "Dress-Up Day" (3-1) "Tuck-in Time for Mom" (3-2)
Book 3-2	"Dress-Up Day" (3-1) "Tuck-in Time for Mom" (3-2) "Follow Your Heart" (4)
Book 4	"Tuck-in Time for Mom" (3-2) "Follow Your Hear" (4) "How to Unearth Earthworms" (5)
Book 5	"Follow Your Heart" (4) "How to Unearth Earthworms" (5) "Trash in the Tides" (6)

Customizing the Test Administration

The levels that you administer will depend on the levels of the reading materials your students have completed. Each student takes three levels of the test. You have the flexibility to "customize" the test for each student or for groups of students.

For example, suppose a fourth-grade teacher is preparing to administer the test to students who were grouped into two ability levels in third grade. The higher-achieving group completed both books of the third grade by the end of last year. They should take levels 3-1, 3-2, and 4. The second group completed the first book of third grade last year. They should take levels 2-2, 3-l, and 3-2. This teacher will use the copying masters found in the Appendix to create two versions of the student booklets. Each ability group in the class will use one of the two versions.

Because the directions and sample items are the same for both versions, both groups can take the test together, even though they will be working on different passages and items. Since one set of common directions and sample items is used for grades 3 through 6, it is even possible to administer the test to students in different grade levels within those groupings at the same time.

Specific Directions For Administering The Placement Test

The directions and samples used for administering the Placement Test are the same for all levels.

Directions For Vocabulary In Context

The Vocabulary in Context subtest should be administered in one sitting. Distribute the Student Booklets. Have each student fill in his or her name, the date, teacher's name, and grade in the space provided on the front cover. Then administer the test according to the directions that follow.

Read the following general directions to the students.

Say: *We are going to take a test to find out how well you can read. Some of the questions will be easy and some will be more difficult. Do your very best, and try to answer all of the questions.*

Say: *Open your test booklet to the sample page, and fold the booklet so that you see only the sample page.*

Make sure that each student is looking at the correct page.

Say: *Look at the top of the sample page. Find the sample sentence that has a blank in it. Under that sentence are four words. You are to find the word that best completes the sentence and fill in the answer circle under the word you choose. Let's work this one together.*

Call on a volunteer to read the sample sentence.

Say: *Which of the words under that sentence would best fill in the blank and complete the sentence?* (**bored**)

Say: *That's correct. **I was bored because I had nothing to do all afternoon.** You should have filled in answer circle **A** under the word **bored**.*

Make sure each student has completed the sample correctly. Help anyone who is having difficulty. If necessary, demonstrate how to fill in the answer circle on the board.

Then say: *Now you are going to work on your own. Turn to page ( ). You are to fill in the answer circle under the word that best completes each sentence. When you come to the end of page ( ), put down your pencil. Sit quietly until everyone has finished. Does everyone understand what you are to do? Remember to keep working until you come to the end of page ( ). Then put down your pencil, and sit quietly until I tell you what to do next. I will write on the board the pages you must complete.*

Write on the board the beginning and ending page numbers for the Vocabulary in Context subtest. Provide help for any student who has difficulty. Check to make sure everyone is on the correct starting page.

Say: *You may begin now.*

Walk around the room and monitor the students as they are working. Allow enough time for students to complete the thirty Vocabulary in Context items that appear in their booklets.

When all students have completed the Vocabulary in Context subtest, collect the test booklets. This concludes the first session.

© Harcourt

Directions For Reading Comprehension

Say: *Open your test booklet to the sample page, and fold the booklet so that you see only the sample page.*

Make sure that each student is looking at the correct page.

Say: *Look at the middle of the sample page. Find the words "Learning About Dolphins." This is the title of the passage. Under the title is a question. The question asks, "What is special about dolphins?" That question will help you understand what the passage is about.*

Now I would like you to read the sample passage. After the passage, there are two questions. You are to read each question and fill in the answer circle in front of the best answer for each question. Then sit quietly until I tell you what to do next.

Allow time for the students to read the passage and answer the questions that follow.

Call on a volunteer to read each question and give the correct response.

Say: *That's correct. The word **communicate** in this passage means "send messages." You should have filled in answer circle **B** in front of the words **send messages**.*

Repeat the process with the second sample question.

Say: *That's correct. Dolphins talk to each other through sounds that they make. You should have filled in answer circle **A** in front of the words **through sounds**.*

Make sure each student has completed the samples correctly. Help anyone who is having difficulty.

Then say: *Now you are going to work on your own. Turn to page ( ). You are to read each passage and the questions that follow. Then fill in the answer circle in front of the correct answer for each question. When you come to the end of page ( ), put down your pencil. Sit quietly until everyone has finished. Does everyone understand what you are to do? Remember to keep working until you come to the end of page ( ). Then put down your pencil, and sit quietly until I tell you what to do next. I will write on the board the pages you must complete.*

Write on the board the beginning and ending page numbers for the Reading Comprehension subtest. Provide help for any student who has difficulty. Check to make sure everyone is on the correct starting test page.

Say: *You may begin now.*

Walk around the room and monitor the students as they are working. Allow enough time for students to read the three passages and complete the twenty-four Reading Comprehension items that appear in their booklets.

When all students have completed the Reading Comprehension subtest, collect the test booklets. This concludes the Placement Test.

Scoring And Interpreting The Placement Test

One point is given for each correct response. Each student will have completed a total of thirty Vocabulary in Context items and twenty-four Reading Comprehension items. These fifty-four test items cover three different program levels—Below Level, On Level, and Above Level.

After students have completed the Placement Test, you can score and record the results in a two-step process.

Step 1: Use the Answer Keys located in this section to score each subtest. Count the number of correct responses, and record this information in the spaces provided on the cover of each student's test booklet ("Pupil Summary of Placement Test Results").

Step 2: In the Appendix you will find a form labeled "Class Summary of Placement Test Results." This form should be used to summarize the Placement Test performance for an entire class. It contains places to record the levels administered, total vocabulary score, total comprehension score, total test score ("Grand Total"), placement level, and comments about each student who took the Placement Test. The following section explains how to determine the placement level from the students' scores.

Answer Keys

Vocabulary in Context

Level 2-1	Level 2-2
1. B	1. C
2. C	2. A
3. A	3. D
4. A	4. B
5. B	5. C
6. B	6. A
7. D	7. B
8. A	8. B
9. B	9. C
10. C	10. D

Level 3-1	Level 3-2	Level 4	Level 5	Level 6
1. C	1. C	1. B	1. B	1. B
2. B	2. A	2. A	2. C	2. C
3. A	3. B	3. B	3. A	3. A
4. C	4. B	4. C	4. B	4. B
5. A	5. A	5. C	5. C	5. D
6. D	6. D	6. D	6. A	6. C
7. A	7. B	7. B	7. C	7. B
8. B	8. D	8. D	8. C	8. A
9. B	9. B	9. B	9. A	9. D
10. C	10. A	10. A	10. A	10. A

Answer Keys

• •

Reading Comprehension

Level 2-1	Level 2-2
Soup or Salad	In the Middle of the Night
1. C	1. C
2. B	2. A
3. D	3. C
4. B	4. B
5. A	5. D
6. C	6. A
7. A	7. B
8. B	8. A

Level 3-1	Level 3-2	Level 4	Level 5	Level 6
Dress-Up Day	Tuck-in Time for Mom	Follow Your Heart	How to Unearth Earthworms	Trash in the Tides
1. B	1. C	1. C	1. B	1. B
2. C	2. A	2. A	2. D	2. C
3. A	3. A	3. D	3. C	3. C
4. D	4. D	4. B	4. A	4. A
5. B	5. B	5. C	5. B	5. C
6. A	6. C	6. A	6. A	6. B
7. C	7. D	7. C	7. C	7. D
8. D	8. A	8. B	8. A	8. B

Determining Placement Levels

A student's total test score (vocabulary and comprehension scores combined) is used to determine the student's placement in the program. Table 3 ("Determining Placement"), has been designed to help you determine a student's appropriate placement and level of support, based on the total test score. To use Table 3, follow these steps:

1. Identify in the left-hand column the level of the reading program the student has just completed.

2. Find in the middle column the student's total test score, or Grand Total, on the Placement Test.

3. Find in the right-hand column the placement and support level that corresponds to the student's total test score. This is the level of suport the student should receive.

The Placement Test results, including placement levels for an entire class, can be summarized on the "Class Summary of Placement Test Results" form located in the Appendix.

For example, suppose that your class just completed Book 3-2 of another program, and you administered items from levels 3-1 (Below Level), 3-2 (On Level), and 4 (Above Level). Look at Table 3 under Book 3-2 (Level Just Completed). Your students will be placed in Book 4 and given "below level" support if they scored 37 or below and "on level" support if they scored between 38 and 50. Any students who earned a score of 51 and above should be given "advanced" level support if they continue to show strong performance.

Examples

Robert Lopez recently completed Book 3-2 in another reading program. He took levels 3-1, 3-2, and 4 of the Placement Test. He scored 28 on the Vocabulary in Context subtest and 20 on the Reading Comprehension subtest. His Grand Total is 48. Because his total score is between 38 and 50, Robert can be placed in Book 4. A note in the "Comments" column serves as a reminder of the type of support Robert should receive.

Like Robert Lopez, Tami Steel also completed Book 3-2 in another program and took levels 3-1, 3-2, and 4 of the Placement Test. She scored 16 on the Vocabulary in Context subtest and 17 on the Reading Comprehension subtest. Her Grand Total is 33. Because her total is below 37, Tami should be placed in Book 4 and given "below level" support.

Student Name	Levels Administered	Total Vocabulary	Total Comprehension	Grand Total	Placement Level	Comments
Robert Lopez	3-1, 3-2, 4	28	20	48	4	On level
Tami Steel	3-1, 3-2, 4	16	17	33	3-2	Below level

If any students score below 37, there is a good chance that they are reading below level. In these cases you should consider further informal testing to determine the best instructional support. At the very least you should observe such students carefully during reading instruction to determine whether the additional support is necessary. The Phonemic Awareness Inventory and the Phonics Inventory are designed for administration to individual students to resolve level of support decisions.

TABLE 3

Determining Placement		
Level Just Completed	**Total Test Score**	**Appropriate Placement Level**
Book 2-2	37 and below 38 to 50 51 and above	Book 3-1 • Below level* • On level • Advanced
Book 3-1	37 and below 38 to 50 51 and above	Book 3-2 • Below level • On level • Advanced
Book 3-2	37 and below 38 to 50 51 and above	Book 4 • Below level • On level • Advanced
Book 4	37 and below 38 to 50 51 and above	Book 5 • Below level • On level • Advanced
Book 5	37 and below 38 to 50 51 and above	Book 6 • Below level • On level • Advanced

* You may wish to administer the Phonemic Awareness Inventory or the Phonics Inventory to students who score at this level to obtain another estimate of their performance and to plan instruction.

The score patterns for each student may be examined to determine whether the student performed as expected. The general pattern is for students to get fewer items correct as they complete more difficult test items. The scores of very poor readers and very good readers may not follow the usual patterns because so few test items are answered either correctly or incorrectly. With poor readers, better performance on the more difficult items may be a matter of chance. Good readers may miss a number of the easier test items because of carelessness.

The score patterns will help you learn more about your students. In some cases, further testing using the Diagnostic Assessments may be necessary to determine the best instructional placement.

Because no single test can ever be a totally valid instructional placement for a child, you should observe your students and their work as you conduct your daily reading program. You will almost certainly want to adjust the instructional placements of some of the students as you learn more about their reading ability.

Field-Test Information

The Placement Test was developed in collaboration with Dr. Roger Farr and the Center for Reading and Language Studies at Indiana University. This Center was chosen because of its wide range of experience in developing language arts assessments.

The Placement Test was written by professional test-development personnel using specifications based on the program. A listing of school test sites that participated in the field tests of assessment components for the program follows.

Field-Test Design

A variety of types of school districts participated in the field tests. They represented different geographic regions of the country, different socioeconomic groups, and different sizes. Participating students represented a broad range of ability levels.

All assessments were administered by regular classroom teachers and returned to Indiana University for scoring and analysis. Standardized directions were provided for each teacher. Suggested test sittings and approximate testing times were provided; however, teachers were encouraged to allow sufficient time for all students to complete the assessments.

Although each reading selection, comprehension question, and vocabulary item was targeted for a particular grade level, the passages and items were tried out at more than one grade level during the field tests to gain a better estimate of item difficulty for students at various grade levels. This type of off-grade testing recognizes the developmental nature of the learning process and facilitates better estimates of item difficulty for students at various grade levels.

Field-Test Data Analysis

The item analysis data included the number and percent of students choosing each response option or omitting the item. Point-biserial item discrimination indices were also calculated for each item by grade level. These item-level statistics formed the primary sets of data used to select the final passages and items and to make appropriate item revisions.

Each participating teacher also completed a questionnaire, indicating the appropriateness of the passages and items, the interest level of the materials, and the clarity of the directions.

Based on the field-test data, the final Placement Test was built by the publisher.

Field-Test Sites

Westwood Elementary
Coker, AL

Huntington Place Elementary
Northport, AL

Englewood Elementary School
Tuscaloosa, AL

North Shore Elementary
Jacksonville, FL

Southside Elementary School
Jacksonville, FL

A. C. Alexander
Kenner, LA

Greenleaf School
Haverill, MA

Tilton School
Haverill, MA

IS 68
Brooklyn, NY

IS 252
Brooklyn, NY

PS 114
Brooklyn, NY

PS 135
Brooklyn, NY

PS 208
Brooklyn, NY

PS 244
Brooklyn, NY

Chase Elementary School
Cincinnati, OH

Millvale Primary School
Cincinnati, OH

Mt. Washington School
Cincinnati, OH

Silverton Paideia School
Cincinnati, OH

Mt. View Elementary School
Greensburg, PA

Latrobe Elementary School
Latrobe, PA

Latrobe Junior High School
Latrobe, PA

Overbrook Educational Center
Philadelphia, PA

Bransford Elementary
Colleyville, TX

O. C. Taylor Elementary
Colleyville, TX

Lockhart Technology Academy
Houston, TX

Scarborough Elementary
Houston, TX

W. G. Love Elementary
Houston, TX

Brookside Intermediate
Webster, TX

Patrick Henry Greene Elementary
Webster, TX

Elizabeth Vaughan Elementary
Woodbridge, VA

Locust Lane Elementary
Eau Claire, WI

Putnam Heights Elementary
Eau Claire, WI

Phonemic Awareness Inventory

Phonemic awareness is an understanding that speech is composed of a series of sounds, or phonemes. Children who have difficulty attending to and manipulating the sounds in their language are likely to have problems learning to read. These children need additional experience with oral language to heighten their sensitivity to the phonemic basis of speech.

Overview of the Phonemic Awareness Inventory

The Phonemic Awareness Inventory is a series of oral tests designed to provide informal assessment of an individual's level of phonemic awareness skills to help the teacher plan instruction. The Phonemic Awareness Inventory consists of the following tasks:

Contents of the Phonemic Awareness Inventory		
Task	Title of Task	Purpose of Task
1	Segmenting Phonemes in a Word	Assesses ability to identify the individual sounds in a spoken word.
2	Deleting Words and Syllables	Assesses ability to delete syllables in compound words and multi-syllabic words.
3	Deleting Phonemes	Assesses ability to delete an individual phoneme in a word and orally produce the remaining part of the word
4	Substituting Initial and Final Sounds	Assesses ability to substitute either an initial or final sound in a spoken word to produce a new word.

General Guidelines for Administering

The Phonemic Awareness Inventory should be conducted individually in a quiet and comfortable setting. By administering the Inventory individually, the teacher can be sure the student is attending to the task and can gain insights into problems the student may be having.

You may use any one, or all, of the tasks. If you wish to obtain a comprehensive understanding of the student's phonemic awareness, administer all four tasks. If you are interested in evaluating a specific aspect of phonemic awareness, administer only those tasks that are relevant to your needs. Whether you administer all tasks or just selected tasks, the tasks should be given in sequential order.

The Phonemic Awareness Inventory covers a range of phonemic skills. Although most students develop phonemic awareness skills in the early grades, other students may not reach proficiency in phonemic awareness until later in the elementary grades. **If a student misses four items in a row, discontinue testing of that particular task and move on to the next task. Also stop testing any time a student displays frustration and obvious discomfort with a task.**

There is no time limit. It will take approximately 15 minutes to administer all four tasks. If possible, the tasks should be administered in a single session.

You and the student should be seated at a flat table or desk. The best seating location for you is facing the student, to facilitate clear diction and immediate recording of responses.

Become familiar with the directions and items. Specific directions for administering each task can be found on each Administering and Recording Form (see Appendix). The text in **bold** type is intended to be read aloud. The other information is for the teacher or examiner only and should not be read aloud. You should feel free to rephrase the directions, to repeat the samples, or to give additional examples to make sure the student understands what to do.

Before beginning the Inventory, spend a few minutes in light, friendly conversation with the child. Don't refer to the Inventory as a "test." Tell the student you would like to play some "word games."

Specific Directions for Administering

Follow these steps to administer the Phonemic Awareness Inventory:

1. Duplicate a copy of the "Administering and Recording Form" for each task you will be administering and one "Summary of Performance" form. You will record a student's responses on the "Administering and Recording Form" and summarize the totals on the "Summary of Performance" form." The student will not need any materials.

2. Explain that the words the student hears and says every day are made up of sounds and that you will be saying some words and sounds and asking questions about them. Be sure to speak clearly.

3. Administer the tasks in sequential order. If the student has difficulty with the first four items or cannot answer them, stop giving that particular task and move on to another.

4. Follow the same basic procedures when administering each task. First, model the task so the student understands what to do. Second, administer the sample item and provide positive feedback to the child. Third, administer the items for that task. Fourth, record the student's responses for each item.

5. After giving the Inventory, record the student's scores on the "Summary of Performance" form. Use the "Performance Level" scale on the Summary Form to determine the level that best describes the student's phonemic awareness.

© Harcourt

Phonics Inventory

Purpose

The Phonics Inventory is designed to assess a student's understanding of sound-symbol relationships and word structure knowledge, and the ability to apply that knowledge. The student is asked to pronounce a series of nonsense words that have been carefully constructed to assess a wide range of phonic and structural elements. By analyzing a student's responses, the teacher can determine specific strengths and weaknesses in phonic and structural analysis and use that information to plan instruction.

Why use nonsense words? Nonsense words are used because they provide a truer measure of a student's decoding skills. If a student is asked to decode real words, the teacher can never be sure if the student read a word correctly because of ability to apply phonic or structural skills, or because the word was in the student's sight vocabulary. Since the nonsense words used on the Phonics Inventory are not in a student's sight vocabulary, the teacher can be certain that the student used phonic and word structure skills to decode the words.

Who should be given the Phonics Inventory? It is probably not necessary to give the Phonics Inventory to all students. Because it must be administered individually, it would take considerable time and effort to administer it to all students in a class. Ideally, the Phonics Inventory should be administered in the following situations:

• To students who are experiencing difficulty and who are reading below grade level

• To students who are at risk of being retained because of inadequate progress in reading

• To new students for whom little information is available from their previous teacher or-school

• To students who have been receiving special reading instruction either inside or outside the regular classroom

Description of the Phonics Inventory

The Phonics Inventory is composed of six sections. Each section consists of ten "items" or ten nonsense words that a student is asked to decode. The sections progress in difficulty from simple CVC pattern words to three- and four-syllable words.

Although a section may focus on one phonic or structural element, by recording and analyzing a student's response, a teacher can gain diagnostic information about other elements as well. For example, Section 2 assesses a student's understanding of consonant blends. However, because the consonant blends are presented in the context of CVC patterns, a teacher can also gain insights into the student's understanding of short vowels as well as initial and final single consonants. The table below summarizes the content of each section.

Contents of the Phonics Inventory	
Section	**Contents**
CVC Words	• initial consonants and single consonants • short medial vowels • final single consonants and consonant blends
Consonant Blends	• initial consonants and consonant blends • short medial vowels • final single consonants and consonant blends
Consonant Digraphs	• initial consonant digraphs • final consonant digraphs • short medial vowels
CVCe Words	• long vowels in the CVCe pattern • initial single consonants • final single consonants
Vowels	• vowel digraphs • vowel diphthongs • r-controlled vowels
Multisyllabic Words	• short vowels in closed syllables (e.g., "dab") • long vowels in open syllables (e.g., "ta") • inflections, prefixes, suffixes

Directions for Using the Phonics Inventory

The Phonics Inventory must be administered individually in a quiet and comfortable setting. The teacher should record a student's responses discreetly as the Inventory is being administered. Some teachers find it helpful to tape the administration of the Inventory because they can return to the audio tape later to verify their scoring.

The teacher and the student should be seated at a flat table or desk. The best seating location for the teacher is facing the student so he or she can clearly hear and record the student's responses.

Before you begin, explain to the student that you want to see how well the student can pronounce words. For example, you could say, *"I'm going to show you some make-believe words and ask you to pronounce them for me. These are not real words, they are make-believe words. Look at each word carefully and try to pronounce it as best you can. I'm going to write down your pronunciations."* Some students become frustrated with nonsense words and attempt to make real words out of them even if it means mispronouncing the word. If this should happen, stop the testing and remind the student that these are nonsense words and it is not necessary to turn them into real words.

Either use the word lists provided in the Appendix or make 3 x 5 inch word cards for each nonsense word on the Phonics Inventory. These cards can be reused each time you administer the Inventory. Make a photocopy of the Student Record Form to use for recording student responses.

Become familiar with the nonsense words on the Inventory and how they should be pronounced. Record a student's responses phonetically, just the way they sound as you are administering the Inventory. Return to the Student Record Form at a later time when the student is not present to check the particular elements the student used correctly.

It may not be necessary to administer the entire Phonics Inventory to each student. For example, if a student shows great difficulty with the first section (CVC Words), a teacher could "spot check" (i.e., administer two or three items) Consonant Blends and Consonant Digraphs, but skip more difficult sections such as Vowels, and Multisyllabic Words. Likewise, if you know a student possesses sound-symbol relationships for most of the consonants and short vowels, you may want to administer only the more advanced sections in the Inventory.

The Phonics Inventory is not a timed test. It will take approximately 20 minutes to administer all six sections of the Inventory depending upon how quickly the student responds. Give a student ample time to respond. Don't rush the student, but if a student is reluctant to attempt a response or labors excessively on item after item, control the pace by moving on to another item. It is possible to administer the Inventory in two or three sessions.

Scoring and Interpreting the Phonics Inventory

Although it is possible to obtain a score for each section of the Phonics Inventory and a total score for the entire Inventory, the true value of the instrument lies in it diagnostic utility.

Assuming that you recorded the student's responses on the Student Record Form as you administered the Inventory, follow the steps below to score and interpret the Inventory:

- For each nonsense word pronounced correctly, place a checkmark next to the student's-pronunciation.
- Record the number of words pronounced correctly in each section in the space provided at the bottom of each section. *A student must pronounce all elements correctly to receive credit.* Scores may range from 0 (none correct) to 10 (all correct).
- Transfer the section scores to the Performance Profile by simply circling the number of-words pronounced correctly in each section. Record observations in the Comments-section.
- Return to the Student Record Form and analyze the student's responses by looking for patterns. For example, does the student show a good understanding of sound-letter relationships for consonants? in both initial and final positions? Does the student display an understanding of vowel patterns (CVC/CVCe)?
- Record the strengths and weaknesses that you observe from your analysis of the student's responses on the Performance Profile and decide on appropriate instructional priorities for the student.

Example

The following example illustrates how to score and interpret the Phonics Inventory. Leslie is in the fourth grade. She moved into her new school in the middle of the school year. After administering the Placement Test, her teacher gave the Phonics Inventory to get a more complete picture of Leslie's decoding skills. Leslie's Performance Profile and Student Record Form can be found on the following pages.

Phonics Inventory
Performance Profile

Name _Leslie_   Date _January_

Section	Number Correct (Circle One)	Comments
1. CVC Words	0 1 2 3 4 5 6 7 8 (9) 10	Excellent with CVC pattern
2. Consonant Blends	0 1 2 3 4 5 6 7 (8) 9 10	Final - pt + ft only ones missed
3. Consonant Digraphs	0 1 2 3 4 5 6 7 (8) 9 10	Knows most con. digraphs
4. Long Vowels	0 1 2 3 4 (5) 6 7 8 9 10	Has difficulty with this pattern
5. Vowels: Digraphs/ Diphthongs/R-Controlled	0 1 2 (3) 4 5 6 7 8 9 10	Great difficulty with these vowels
6. Multisyllabic Words	0 (1) 2 3 4 5 6 7 8 9 10	Good attempt but weakness in vowels
Total Score		hampers multisyllabic analysis.

Strengths: _Leslie has a great foundation. Knows consonants, digraphs and blends + CVC (short vowel) patterns_

Weaknesses: _Major weakness with Vowels — long in CVCe pattern + digraphs, diphthongs, and r-controlled_

Instructional Priorities: _Focus on Vowels; Word structure (prefixes, suffixes), and multisyllabic words._

Phonics Inventory
Recording Form

Name _Leslie_   Date _January_

CVC Words
Response
1. bem _bem_
2. sab _sab_
3. nid _nid_
4. kon _kone_
5. fip _fip_
6. jeg _jeg_
7. lob _lob_
8. tat _tat_
9. vud _vud_
10. gen _gen_

Score _9_

Consonant Blends
Response
1. clup _clup_ ✓
2. drat _drat_ ✓
3. flem _flem_ ✓
4. stim _stim_ ✓
5. grud _grud_ ✓
6. nast _nast_ ✓
7. lipt _lip_
8. mesk _mesk_ ✓
9. reft _ref_
10. pund _pund_ ✓

Score _8_

Consonant Digraphs
Response
1. shan _shan_ ✓
2. chas _chas_ ✓
3. thib _thib_ ✓
4. whem _whem_ ✓
5. phat _pat_
6. fong _fong_ ✓
7. rath _rath_ ✓
8. seck _sick_
9. resh _resh_ ✓
10. fitch _fitch_ ✓

Score _8_

CVCe Words
Response
1. nobe _nob_
2. rafe _raf_
3. tife _tife_ ✓
4. dute _dute_ ✓
5. lope _lope_ ✓
6. bame _bam_
7. kote _kote_ ✓
8. nate _nat_
9. faine _fin_
10. breeme _breeme_ ✓

Score _5_

Vowels: Digraphs/ Diphthongs/R-Control
Response
1. neap _nep_
2. doil _doll_
3. sook _sook_ ✓
4. yaw _yaw_ ✓
5. bir _bar_
6. zart _zirt_
7. zowl _zowling_
8. noy _noy_ ✓
9. tout _toot_
10. gooze _gooey_

Score _3_

Multisyllabic Words
Response
1. dabbet (dab-bet) _dab-bet_ ✓
2. pelrim (pel-rim) _pee-rim_
3. ziptod (zip-tod) _zip-toad_
4. tabert (ta-bert) _tab-bert_
5. jusold (ju-sold) _just-old_
6. fokay (fo-kay) _for-kay_
7. bicturing (bic-tur-ing) _bicture_
8. sackbility (sack-bil-i-ty) _sack-_
9. canberize (can-ber-ize) _canberry_
10. trofounds (tro-founds) _trofund_

Score _1_

© Harcourt

Appendix: Copying Masters

. . . .

StoryTown

Pupil Summary of
Placement Test Results

Name _____   Date _____

Teacher _____   Grade _____

Levels Administered	Vocabulary	Comprehension
_____	_____/10	_____/8
_____	_____/10	_____/8
_____	_____/10	_____/8
Totals	_____/30	_____/24 Grand Total _____/54

Placement Level _____

Vocabulary in Context

1. I was _____ because I had nothing to do all afternoon.

bored	powerful	yesterday	clever
Ⓐ	Ⓑ	Ⓒ	Ⓓ

Reading Comprehension

Learning About Dolphins
What is special about dolphins?

Did you know that dolphins "talk" to each other? Many scientists think that dolphins are among the world's most intelligent creatures. They send messages, or <u>communicate</u>, to each other by making unusual sounds that often seem like clicks or whistles. Many scientists believe dolphins make different sounds at different times, such as when they are in trouble and when they are playing. Someday scientists hope to better understand the messages that these interesting mammals send to each other.

1. The word *communicate* in this passage means _____ .

argue	send messages	play	give help
Ⓐ	Ⓑ	Ⓒ	Ⓓ

2. How do dolphins "talk" to each other?
Ⓐ through sounds
Ⓑ by flapping their fins
Ⓒ by leaping out of the water
Ⓓ through unusual swimming patterns

© Harcourt

3

1. He had a good _____ to be happy.

   clay   reason   braid   pound

   Ⓐ   Ⓑ   Ⓒ   Ⓓ

2. We saw animals when we walked in the _____.

   time   work   woods   rock

   Ⓐ   Ⓑ   Ⓒ   Ⓓ

3. Grandmother _____ roses in the flower bed.

   planted   rained   washed   molded

   Ⓐ   Ⓑ   Ⓒ   Ⓓ

4. Max looks very _____ today.

   handsome   from   again   called

   Ⓐ   Ⓑ   Ⓒ   Ⓓ

5. I handed my dad a _____ to fix the car.

   hole   tool   frog   lake

   Ⓐ   Ⓑ   Ⓒ   Ⓓ

6. Everything is just _____ !

says   perfect   own   always

Ⓐ   Ⓑ   Ⓒ   Ⓓ

7. Drink your milk so you will grow big and _____.

hot   quiet   slow   strong

Ⓐ   Ⓑ   Ⓒ   Ⓓ

8. Snakes _____ their skin at certain times of the year.

shed   surround   discover   follow

Ⓐ   Ⓑ   Ⓒ   Ⓓ

9. The mother bear _____ her baby from other animals.

opens   protects   lives   laughs

Ⓐ   Ⓑ   Ⓒ   Ⓓ

10. Keisha lives in a small _____.

glass   friend   village   promise

Ⓐ   Ⓑ   Ⓒ   Ⓓ

1. Was that book fun to read, or was it _____ ?

going   facing   boring   stating

Ⓐ   Ⓑ   Ⓒ   Ⓓ

2. Yes, I _____ you could go with me.

suppose   same   shine   wrong

Ⓐ   Ⓑ   Ⓒ   Ⓓ

3. My dog likes it when I _____ his head.

should   rave   dance   stroke

Ⓐ   Ⓑ   Ⓒ   Ⓓ

4. You look pretty in that _____ green color.

tame   pale   large   across

Ⓐ   Ⓑ   Ⓒ   Ⓓ

5. That man is the _____ of the train.

nail   tray   conductor   stone

Ⓐ   Ⓑ   Ⓒ   Ⓓ

© Harcourt

6. Place that heavy box on this _____ table.

   sturdy   closely   pretty   sickly

   Ⓐ   Ⓑ   Ⓒ   Ⓓ

7. I am sorry I _____ you to fall down.

   stocked   caused   been   went

   Ⓐ   Ⓑ   Ⓒ   Ⓓ

8. I went to the city to see my _____.

   mist   relatives   stop   nothing

   Ⓐ   Ⓑ   Ⓒ   Ⓓ

9. I want to thank you for your kind _____.

   board   cloud   hospitality   morning

   Ⓐ   Ⓑ   Ⓒ   Ⓓ

10. We watched the birds _____ through the air.

   buy   thank   miss   glide

   Ⓐ   Ⓑ   Ⓒ   Ⓓ

Vocabulary in Context

1. I _____ a bug crawling on the blanket.

   threw   spoiled   noticed   respected

   (A)   (B)   (C)   (D)

2. Trish _____ enough money to buy a new bicycle.

   planted   earned   rowed   smeared

   (A)   (B)   (C)   (D)

3. This is an _____ surprise!

   unexpected   around   asked   imagination

   (A)   (B)   (C)   (D)

4. We followed the _____ through the forest.

   omelet   hole   trail   coal

   (A)   (B)   (C)   (D)

5. When I give _____ , my dog always does what I say.

   commands   likes   pairs   parks

   (A)   (B)   (C)   (D)

6. I sent her a _____ telling her to wait for me.

   mountain   coast   mouse   message

   (A)   (B)   (C)   (D)

7. We were as _____ about our new teacher as he was about us.

   curious   strong   lazy   found

   (A)   (B)   (C)   (D)

8. Stop talking and pay _____ to the teacher.

   comfort   attention   program   message

   (A)   (B)   (C)   (D)

9. We did not know if we could _____ before the storm hit.

   always   escape   please   next

   (A)   (B)   (C)   (D)

10. The doctor wrote a _____ for me when I was sick.

    birthday   breakfast   prescription   pride

    (A)   (B)   (C)   (D)

Vocabulary in Context

1. We lay in the grass, _____ up at the clouds.

   changing   trapping   gazing   shaking

   (A)   (B)   (C)   (D)

2. The worker felt _____ after spending eight hours in the hot sun.

   weary   skillful   illuminated   tender

   (A)   (B)   (C)   (D)

3. A cat is _____ loudly outside my window.

   meeting   wailing   missing   biting

   (A)   (B)   (C)   (D)

4. My teacher always gives me good _____.

   along   advice   past   rain

   (A)   (B)   (C)   (D)

5. The waters of the lake _____ in the sun like silver.

   glistened   pointed   laughed   rode

   (A)   (B)   (C)   (D)

6. I caught the biggest fish in the whole _____.

   carrot   color   clown   county

   (A)   (B)   (C)   (D)

7. Suki _____ the rope tightly as she led the horse down the path.

   cooked   clutched   crawled   cared

   (A)   (B)   (C)   (D)

8. The teacher will _____ our test scores to get our final grades.

   stray   receive   harvest   average

   (A)   (B)   (C)   (D)

9. The climbers will attempt to reach the _____ by Friday.

   bid   peak   profit   value

   (A)   (B)   (C)   (D)

10. When the fruit is ripe, we will _____ it.

    harvest   heard   hello   smile

    (A)   (B)   (C)   (D)

Vocabulary in Context

1. The boys played ball in the _____ lot across the street.

satisfied	vacant	anxious	uneasy
Ⓐ	Ⓑ	Ⓒ	Ⓓ

2. My uncle gets paid a good _____ for his work.

salary	pageant	meadow	match
Ⓐ	Ⓑ	Ⓒ	Ⓓ

3. In art class, we painted a _____ on the classroom wall.

bravery	mural	routine	danger
Ⓐ	Ⓑ	Ⓒ	Ⓓ

4. The runner _____ to a stop at first base.

announced	hounded	skidded	answered
Ⓐ	Ⓑ	Ⓒ	Ⓓ

5. It is better to forgive than to hold a _____ against someone.

trader	wonder	grudge	rehearsal
Ⓐ	Ⓑ	Ⓒ	Ⓓ

6. "I'm happy to make your _____ ," the new student said to me.

spirit	chortle	disappointment	acquaintance
Ⓐ	Ⓑ	Ⓒ	Ⓓ

7. She has an _____ for the time the crime took place.

ingredient	alibi	invention	announcer
Ⓐ	Ⓑ	Ⓒ	Ⓓ

8. If the plan is not _____ to you, we will make a new plan.

sickly	scoured	restless	acceptable
Ⓐ	Ⓑ	Ⓒ	Ⓓ

9. We opened all the windows to _____ the building.

adore	ventilate	retire	stagger
Ⓐ	Ⓑ	Ⓒ	Ⓓ

10. We heard a bull _____ in a nearby meadow.

bellowing	sprucing	recognizing	driving
Ⓐ	Ⓑ	Ⓒ	Ⓓ

© Harcourt

Vocabulary in Context

1. This shell is a _____ I brought back from the beach.

   commotion   souvenir   wave   language

   (A)   (B)   (C)   (D)

2. Working all day left the boys feeling _____.

   stranded   frightened   exhausted   ridiculed

   (A)   (B)   (C)   (D)

3. The small boat _____ violently during the storm at sea.

   pitched   recognized   burrowed   brushed

   (A)   (B)   (C)   (D)

4. I was _____ with joy when our lost dog came home.

   forlorn   overcome   anxious   courageous

   (A)   (B)   (C)   (D)

5. The surface of the planet is _____ and lacks vegetation.

   dedicated   bountiful   barren   gorged

   (A)   (B)   (C)   (D)

6. Our supplies _____ down until we had almost nothing left.

   dwindled   bustled   fielded   generated

   (A)   (B)   (C)   (D)

7. I decided to _____ more time to my studies.

   tread   guess   devote   bolt

   (A)   (B)   (C)   (D)

8. It is an _____ fact that warm air rises.

   answered   earned   undeniable   overdue

   (A)   (B)   (C)   (D)

9. She was so _____ in her work that she didn't hear the bell.

   absorbed   thrived   invented   grimaced

   (A)   (B)   (C)   (D)

10. My aunt works as a Spanish language _____.

   interpreter   nutrition   harness   movie

   (A)   (B)   (C)   (D)

© Harcourt

Vocabulary in Context

1. He should do well in business because he has a _____ mind.

   weak   shrewd   disappointed   pared

   Ⓐ   Ⓑ   Ⓒ   Ⓓ

2. Stella _____ through her closet to find something to wear.

   funded   reacted   rummaged   aced

   Ⓐ   Ⓑ   Ⓒ   Ⓓ

3. The playful cat _____ on the ball of yarn.

   pounced   resembled   bulged   despaired

   Ⓐ   Ⓑ   Ⓒ   Ⓓ

4. The herd dog went _____ after the stray cattle, eager to bring them home.

   perching   charging   distributing   thriving

   Ⓐ   Ⓑ   Ⓒ   Ⓓ

5. The ancient ruins were in good condition because they had been carefully-_____.

   glared   wailed   postponed   preserved

   Ⓐ   Ⓑ   Ⓒ   Ⓓ

6. We were absolutely _____ by the wonders we saw.

   tapered   crested   astounded   wavered

   Ⓐ   Ⓑ   Ⓒ   Ⓓ

7. We stayed in a _____ village that was fifty miles from any other town.

   reluctant   remote   brisk   disdainful

   Ⓐ   Ⓑ   Ⓒ   Ⓓ

8. With _____ less than 500 feet, the pilot could barely see the runway.

   visibility   glare   instinct   migration

   Ⓐ   Ⓑ   Ⓒ   Ⓓ

9. Shelly waved her arms _____ as she tried to get our attention.

   currently   lazily   formally   dramatically

   Ⓐ   Ⓑ   Ⓒ   Ⓓ

10. The astronaut tried to _____ the spacecraft into docking position.

    maneuver   browse   console   issue

    Ⓐ   Ⓑ   Ⓒ   Ⓓ

Soup or Salad?

by Eve Stone

What happened to Rabbit's plans?

One day Rabbit said, "I will make some soup for my friend Chipmunk." He went to his garden to pick some vegetables. He picked some carrots and put them in his wheelbarrow. He picked some tomatoes and put them in his wheelbarrow. He picked peppers and peas and potatoes and put them in his wheelbarrow.

Then Rabbit pushed his wheelbarrow down the <u>path</u>. He was so busy thinking about his soup that he did not notice the big hole in the path. The wheelbarrow hit the hole and tossed the vegetables into the air.

They landed all over the garden. Rabbit looked around. "Well, maybe Chipmunk would like tossed salad instead," he said as he gathered up the vegetables.

1. Rabbit wants to make something for his _____.
   A) mother
   B) father
   C) friend
   D) sister

2. What does Rabbit want to make?
   A) cake
   B) soup
   C) bread
   D) cookies

3. Rabbit went to his garden to pick some _____.
   A) plums
   B) flowers
   C) apples
   D) vegetables

4. Where did Rabbit put the things he picked from his garden?
   A) in a basket
   B) in a wheelbarrow
   C) in a bag
   D) in a box

5. What else might Rabbit pick in his garden?

Ⓐ corn

Ⓑ cheese

Ⓒ fish

Ⓓ milk

6. A <u>path</u> is like a small _____.

Ⓐ river

Ⓑ forest

Ⓒ road

Ⓓ hill

7. After the wheelbarrow turned over, what did Rabbit think he might make?

Ⓐ tossed salad

Ⓑ a sandwich

Ⓒ soup

Ⓓ ice cream

8. This story is silly because rabbits do **not** _____.

Ⓐ look around

Ⓑ have wheelbarrows

Ⓒ eat carrots

Ⓓ hop around

In the Middle of the Night

by George Edward Stanley

What is making the noises in Mary Margaret's room?

In the middle of the night Mary Margaret opened her eyes. She had heard a funny noise in her room. What could it be?

She turned on her lamp. Then she got out of bed and put on her robe and slippers.

First she looked behind her door. But all she found was her teddy bear. So that is where he has been hiding, she thought. She picked him up and set him down in a little rocking chair.

Then she looked inside her closet. But all she found was a <u>pile</u> of dirty clothes. Her mother had told her to put them in the hamper, but she had forgotten. Mary Margaret picked up the clothes and put them in the hamper. Then she heard the noise again.

She looked under her bed. That's where she should have looked in the first place. That's where she found the dragon!

It was sound asleep. It also was snoring loudly. But it looked so comfortable that she couldn't ask it to leave.

Mary Margaret thought for a minute. Then she shook the dragon's shoulder. The dragon opened its sleepy eyes and looked at her.

"If you are going to sleep in my room, you will have to be quieter," Mary Margaret said. "OK?"

The dragon nodded its head. Then it closed its eyes again.

Mary Margaret put one of her pillows under the dragon's head and covered it up with one of her blankets.

Then she took off her robe and slippers, got back into bed, turned off the lamp, and went back to sleep.

1. This story is mostly about a little girl who _____.
- Ⓐ cleans up her room
- Ⓑ gets a new robe
- Ⓒ finds a surprise
- Ⓓ plays with her teddy bear

2. The word <u>pile</u> in the story means _____.
- Ⓐ stack
- Ⓑ chair
- Ⓒ paper
- Ⓓ glass

3. Mary Margaret gets out of bed because she _____.
- Ⓐ needs a drink
- Ⓑ is called by Mother
- Ⓒ hears a noise
- Ⓓ is going to school

4. Where does Mary Margaret find the dragon?
- Ⓐ behind the door
- Ⓑ under her bed
- Ⓒ in the closet
- Ⓓ in her chair

5. The dragon is _____.

   Ⓐ breathing fire

   Ⓑ making the room shake

   Ⓒ wearing Mary Margaret's shoes

   Ⓓ sleeping

6. What does Mary Margaret do to the dragon?

   Ⓐ lets it stay

   Ⓑ pours water on it

   Ⓒ tells it to leave

   Ⓓ runs away from it

7. We can tell Mary Margaret is not afraid of the dragon because she _____.

   Ⓐ feeds it some cake

   Ⓑ gives it a pillow

   Ⓒ takes it to school

   Ⓓ lets it play with her toys

8. Which of these could *not* really happen?

   Ⓐ Mary Margaret finds a dragon in her room.

   Ⓑ She looks inside her closet.

   Ⓒ Mary Margaret puts on her robe.

   Ⓓ She turns on her lamp.

Dress-Up Day

by Maureen Temple

Why did Kerri like to dress up?

Kerri liked to get dressed up.

In the corner of her bedroom there was a large trunk which had been her mother's. The trunk was filled with beautiful clothes for Kerri. Some of them had once been her mother's. Some they had bought at garage sales. And some were extra special because they had been made just for Kerri.

On Saturday morning Kerri cleaned her room or watched television or helped her mother, but she thought about the trunk in the corner of her room.

She thought about the trunk when she ate lunch and when she played outside on Saturday afternoon.

Sometimes Kerri and her mother went shopping on Saturday, and sometimes they bought new clothes. But all the time they were shopping, Kerri thought about the dress-up trunk.

Then just before supper, Kerri's mother would nod to her.

"Why don't you get dressed up for supper, Kerri?" her mother would say.

Kerri would run to her room and open the trunk.

Inside the trunk were all kinds of clothes. Sometimes Kerri was a cowboy or an astronaut or a race-car driver. Sometimes she was a nurse or a doctor or someone bringing mail to the house.

Kerri's daddy was always surprised when she came to the table. "Who is this strange person here?" he would ask.

Kerri would giggle.

"Where's my little girl?"

Kerri would giggle.

Then her father would talk to her as though she were a guest.

If she were a cowboy, he would talk about what it was like to ride horses across the <u>prairie</u>.

If she were a fairy princess, he would talk about moonlight and magic.

Kerri would giggle.

Her daddy could talk about going into space or looking after sick people or being a movie star or driving a race car. He knew just how hard it was to carry a sack full of mail or to be a queen and rule a million people.

But best of all was Saturday night after dinner.

Kerri would have a bath, and her mother would let her use the best powder, and Kerri would put on a clean soft nightgown.

Then she would find her daddy, and she would climb onto his lap. He would hold her close and kiss her.

"Mmmmmm," he would say. "You smell good enough to eat."

Kerri would giggle.

Then he would hug her.

"We always have the best company on Saturday nights," her daddy would say. "I enjoy having these strange people visit me."

And Kerri would giggle because she felt so warm and happy.

"But I'm always glad to have my own little girl back home again," her daddy would say.

And Kerri would giggle.

1. This story is mostly about playing _____.
- Ⓐ school
- Ⓑ dress-up
- Ⓒ cowboys
- Ⓓ baseball

2. What did Kerri think about all Saturday morning and afternoon?
- Ⓐ going shopping
- Ⓑ watching television
- Ⓒ the trunk
- Ⓓ cleaning her room

3. The word <u>trunk</u> in this story means _____.
- Ⓐ a place to keep clothes
- Ⓑ part of an elephant
- Ⓒ part of a tree
- Ⓓ part of a car

4. Kerri liked to get dressed up for _____.
- Ⓐ breakfast
- Ⓑ lunch
- Ⓒ school
- Ⓓ supper

5. How do you know Father liked to play dress-up with Kerri?

Ⓐ He watched television with her.

Ⓑ He talked to her as if she were a stranger.

Ⓒ He took her shopping.

Ⓓ He bought toys for her.

6. The word prairie in this story means _____.

Ⓐ field

Ⓑ street

Ⓒ lake

Ⓓ store

7. What did Kerri do after dinner on Saturday night?

Ⓐ cleaned her room

Ⓑ dressed up like a nurse

Ⓒ sat on her father's lap

Ⓓ watched television

8. How do you think Kerri feels about Saturdays?

Ⓐ angry

Ⓑ sad

Ⓒ lost

Ⓓ happy

Tuck-in Time for Mom

by Patricia M. LeRoy

How do the children help their mom go to sleep?

From the den where Dad watched television, Katie heard the start of the five o'clock news. "Come on, Brian. It's tuck-in time," she called.

Katie grabbed books. Brian grabbed Teddy. They raced down the hallway.

"Knock, knock," Brian yelled as they dashed into Mom's bedroom.

"It's tuck-in time," Katie sang.

Mom was writing at her desk. "Already? Five more minutes," she begged.

Brian shook his head. "You have to go to bed NOW, Mom. You have to get some sleep before you go to work tonight."

"Just two more minutes? Please?"

"We'll read you bedtime stories," Katie offered.

"Bedtime stories? In that case . . ." Mom pushed back her chair and headed for the bed.

As Mom settled under the covers, Katie and Brian climbed on top and nestled beside her.

"I'll read," said Brian. He pulled the red book from the pile. "Stay away from my cave in Tangle-wood Forest!" he growled, pointing to the picture of a mean-looking troll. Mom pulled the blanket over her mouth, then over her eyes. When Brian finished the story, Mom was a lump under the blanket.

"Come out! Come out!" he called, peeling back the blanket.

"No! The scary monster will eat me."

"Here. Teddy will chase the monster."

As Mom clutched Teddy, Brian whispered, "You're only pretend scared, right?"

"Now I'll read," said Katie. "Wendel, the naughty ghost . . ."

"A ghost!" Mom flipped Teddy up, and he landed in Brian's lap.

"A FUNNY ghost. Here, look. Can you find him?" Katie held out the book and Mom pointed.

"Noooo! That's a plant," Katie said. "Try again. Nope, that's a cat." Katie laughed. "Mom! Stop teasing. Right! There's Wendel." Katie turned the page. "Now where's Wendel?"

Mom pointed and yawned.

"The end," said Katie. She fluffed the pillow and tucked the blankets around Mom. Brian slipped Teddy under the blankets.

"All tucked in, Mom? Snug as a bug?" Katie asked.

"Where's my hug?" cried Mom.

Katie and Brian hugged Mom hard.

"Remember to count the stars when you leave for work," Katie reminded. Mom didn't answer.

Brian put his nose to Mom's. "Yup! She's sleeping." He slid off the bed.

"'Night, Mom. We love you," they whispered. They tiptoed across the room, and Katie gently closed the door.

1. This story is mostly about _____.
  - Ⓐ what Dad watches on television
  - Ⓑ where the mother works
  - Ⓒ how the children put their mother to bed
  - Ⓓ what kinds of stories the children tell their mother

2. What time is tuck-in time for mom?
  - Ⓐ 5:00
  - Ⓑ 7:00
  - Ⓒ 9:00
  - Ⓓ 10:00

3. The word begged in the story means _____.
  - Ⓐ asked
  - Ⓑ watched
  - Ⓒ paid
  - Ⓓ pushed

4. In the sentence "You have to go to bed NOW," big letters are used to write NOW to show that _____.
  - Ⓐ Brian's mom is tired
  - Ⓑ Brian's mother has trouble hearing
  - Ⓒ it is the beginning of the sentence
  - Ⓓ Brian says it with strong feelings

5. Mom has to get to sleep because she _____.

   Ⓐ has puffy eyes

   Ⓑ needs rest before she goes to work

   Ⓒ needs rest before she goes on vacation

   Ⓓ has not been feeling well

6. The children get their mother to go to bed by _____.

   Ⓐ promising to let her stay up late tomorrow

   Ⓑ telling her she can watch television in bed

   Ⓒ promising to read her bedtime stories

   Ⓓ telling her she will get a present

7. The story that Brian tells is _____.

   Ⓐ funny

   Ⓑ sad

   Ⓒ mean

   Ⓓ scary

8. Tomorrow night when the evening news comes on, Katie and Brian will probably _____.

   Ⓐ tuck Mom into bed again

   Ⓑ go to school

   Ⓒ fix supper for dad

   Ⓓ write at Mom's desk

Follow Your Heart
by Geary Smith

What do Okno and his son learn?

Okno the Eskimo and his son <u>hitched up</u> their team of sled dogs and took the fish they had caught to the trading post. Okno's son sat in the back of the sled to make sure everything stayed in place. On the way, they met a group of hunters.

"Look at that," one hunter said. "The son is riding, and the father has to walk. What a lazy boy! Since he is younger, he should walk and his father should ride."

Okno and his son traded places. Okno sat in the sled while his son walked, leading the sled dogs. Soon they met some women returning from town.

"Can you believe that?" one asked. "There is a strong man riding in comfort, while his poor little son has to walk."

"I know what to do," replied Okno. "Since the sled is big enough for two people, we both shall ride."

So they did. Okno and his son continued on their way, riding in the sled while the dogs pulled them along. Soon they met some children.

"Look at Okno and his son," the children cried, angry. "They rode all this way, across the ice and snow, while those poor dogs did all the work. How cruel!"

"The children are right," said Okno's son. "We should let the dogs ride in the back while we pull the sled." So they did.

Not long after, Okno and his son met several friends.

"You are both silly!" the friends said, laughing. "You are pulling the dogs when they should be pulling you. You could have been riding in comfort all day!" The friends walked away, laughing and shaking their heads.

Okno's son turned to him. "What do we do now?" he asked.

"From the moment we started on our journey," said Okno, "others have told us what to do, and we listened. But since you can never please all people all of the time, it is best to do what you feel is right in your heart."

So Okno and his son finished their trip by taking turns riding in the sled.

And when they arrived at the trading post, Okno was rested . . . his son was rested. and so were the sled dogs.

1. This story is mostly about _____.
- Ⓐ how to ride a sled in comfort
- Ⓑ winning a dog sled race
- Ⓒ doing what is right in your heart
- Ⓓ taking fish to a trading post

2. The words <u>hitched up</u> in this story mean _____.
- Ⓐ attached
- Ⓑ loosened
- Ⓒ studied
- Ⓓ answered

3. Okno and his son were going _____.
- Ⓐ to the dog sled races
- Ⓑ fishing
- Ⓒ hunting
- Ⓓ to the trading post

4. Okno and his son traded places the **first** time because _____.
- Ⓐ the dogs needed more exercise
- Ⓑ a hunter told them they should
- Ⓒ some children said the dogs were tired
- Ⓓ Okno thought his son was being lazy

5. Friends laughed when the dogs rode in the sled because _____.

    Ⓐ   Okno told a funny joke

    Ⓑ   the dogs did tricks

    Ⓒ   Okno and his son were doing all the work

    Ⓓ   they thought that Okno and his son were lazy

6. Every time Okno and his son met other people, Okno and his son would _____.

    Ⓐ   change places to please the other people

    Ⓑ   have to give the people a gift

    Ⓒ   invite the people to eat with them

    Ⓓ   talk too much and wind up being late

7. How did Okno and his son finish their trip?

    Ⓐ   Okno rode in the sled.

    Ⓑ   The son rode in the sled.

    Ⓒ   They took turns riding in the sled.

    Ⓓ   Okno pulled his son and the dogs in the sled.

8. Which lesson can best be learned from this story?

    Ⓐ   You can't teach an old dog new tricks.

    Ⓑ   You can't please everyone, so please yourself.

    Ⓒ   Always treat older people with respect.

    Ⓓ   Slow and steady wins the race.

How to Unearth Earthworms

by Kathleen Place

How would you unearth an earthworm?

Suppose you want to go on a <u>night crawler</u> hunt. Maybe you'd like to study them or catch them for fishing bait. You can think that there are three parts to hunting these big earthworms.

The first part is to find them. Where? A night crawler is found where soil is moist. Your own backyard is fine. Or you might try a park.

When should you start your search? Try a warm, damp evening after a light rain. Wait until it's dark, and take a flashlight. You will likely find the night crawlers on the surface, partly out of their burrows.

The second problem is how to catch them. They have built-in warning systems to protect themselves. Here's how they work: You spot a night crawler with your flashlight. You run to snatch it. Zip! It goes down its burrow. It has neither eyes nor ears, so how did it know you were there? You probably triggered one or two alarms in its warning system.

One alarm is set off by sensing changes in light. Your flashlight gave the worm a warning. You can fool it by stretching a piece of red cellophane over the top of the flashlight. The worm is not sensitive to red light, but your eyes are.

The second alarm is tripped by your running. A night crawler's body is sensitive to the ground's slightest tremble. If you tiptoe, you will have a better chance of success.

Usually a night crawler lies only partway out of its burrow. If you pull hard, chances are you'll get only a piece of it. Don't worry. A night crawler's body has about 150 rings called <u>segments</u>. If it loses a few from the back end, it can grow new ones.

© Harcourt

The night crawler will play tug-of-war with you by holding onto the sides of the burrow with the help of eight tiny bristles on each segment. If it has 150 segments, that's 1,200 little feet holding fast to the burrow. Grasp it with your whole fist and pull firmly and steadily until it tires and gives up.

After you have caught your worms, the third part is to keep them alive. Carry a can of damp soil with you. Later you can add wet leaves or leaf mold for the worms to munch.

If you plan to fish, you'll have better luck with live bait. If you are going to study them, you'll want to return them to the soil. Worms leave behind castings, bits of unused food that make the soil rich for new plants to grow.

Nature has given worms ways to escape their hunters. But if you can master the problems of finding, catching, and keeping them, you're ready to unearth some earthworms.

1. This story is mostly about _____.
  Ⓐ choosing different types of fish bait
  Ⓑ finding and catching earthworms
  Ⓒ playing tug-of-war
  Ⓓ taking a trip to the park

2. A night crawler in this passage is a big _____.
  Ⓐ spider
  Ⓑ toad
  Ⓒ lizard
  Ⓓ earthworm

3. A good place to find a night crawler is in _____.
  Ⓐ a tree
  Ⓑ the desert
  Ⓒ your backyard
  Ⓓ your house

4. Night crawlers have built-in alarms so that they can _____.
  Ⓐ escape danger
  Ⓑ catch fish
  Ⓒ dig better
  Ⓓ wake up on time

5. One way to fool a night crawler is to _____.

  Ⓐ wear dark clothing

  Ⓑ put red cellophane over your flashlight

  Ⓒ crawl on the ground

  Ⓓ whisper

6. The word segements in this passage _____.

  Ⓐ rings

  Ⓑ hunters

  Ⓒ times

  Ⓓ colors

7. Which question is **not** answered in this passage?

  Ⓐ Where should you look for earthworms?

  Ⓑ How do you catch earthworms?

  Ⓒ How long do most earthworms live?

  Ⓓ What should you do to keep earthworms alive?

8. This story was probably written to _____.

  Ⓐ teach you something

  Ⓑ make you laugh

  Ⓒ frighten you

  Ⓓ make you angry

Trash in the Tides

by Chris Dietel

What can you do to help the trash problem?

One day while walking on the beach, I saw a sea gull that couldn't close his beak. When I moved a little closer, I saw a plastic six-pack holder wrapped around the sea gull's neck and in its beak. How had *that* happened? I tried to catch the sea gull to help it, but it flew away.

Later, I found that all sorts of plastic <u>debris</u> litters our coasts and harms our wildlife. Each year fish, turtles, millions of sea birds, and thousands of sea mammals get caught in plastic cups, bags, straps, rope, lids, toys, fishing line, and more.

Sometimes people litter the beaches, but that is only part of the problem. Ocean ships dump millions of tons of trash into the open sea each year, because it is cheaper and easier than bringing the trash to land. The trash often mixes with currents that carry it to the coasts.

Much of the trash ending up on our coasts is plastic, because we use plastic more than ever before. It is strong, lightweight, and inexpensive. Plastic doesn't decay as fast as paper, wood, or food. Some will stay around for hundreds of years. And most of it floats, so it is easily carried by currents until it ends up on the world's beaches.

The plastic in the currents takes animals by surprise. Unsuspecting fish swim into plastic bags, six-pack holders, and lost plastic fishing nets. Hungry birds dive for the fish, only to get trapped themselves. Curious seals, which may see plastic, poke around plastic rings and packing bands. If they get caught on them, they can die.

Sometimes sea animals mistake plastic for food. Sea turtles have been known to swallow up to fifteen plastic garbage bags, mistaking them for their favorite food, jellyfish. Then, unable to eat, the turtles starve. Whales also eat garbage bags. Once, a whale was found with fifty bags in its stomach. Some fish eat plastic, and when bones of fish-eating birds are found on beaches, they are often mixed with plastic that the fish have eaten. Learning this made me think of the sea gull I had seen wrapped in the six-pack holder. On the beach I once saw some wet plastic near a dead fish, and I noticed that the shiny scales of the fish looked a lot like the wet plastic. Could the sea gull have pecked at the six-pack holder, thinking it was part of a fish?

Fortunately, something is being done to fight the plastics problem on our coasts. In 1988 an international treaty made it illegal to dump plastics at sea. Special plastics are now being made that will decompose more easily. At least twelve states require that plastic six-pack holders eventually break down in sunlight. Other states may soon have this rule.

You can help, too. If you're on a boat or a beach, keep your trash with you until you can dispose of it properly. Cut up six-pack holders before throwing them away. Don't throw plastic into toilets. Even when sewage is treated before its release into the ocean, the plastic will travel with it.

One way to reduce the dangers to coastal wildlife and have fun, too, is to help clean up a beach. Each September and October, the Coastal States Organization sponsors Coastweeks, a two-week celebration that includes a coastal cleanup. Volunteers scout the beaches, collecting loads of trash, especially plastic. One year, eleven thousand volunteers in Florida picked up 270 tons. Some Coastweeks volunteers keep a record of the kinds of trash they find. They send the data to the Center for Marine Conservation, a national organization that is concerned about the oceans. People at the Center study the data, looking for clues about who is doing the littering.

In California, school kids have gotten involved in a program called Adopt-a-Beach. Each member school "adopts" a beach. Some kids take a two-hour bus ride to go clean up their beach.

It wasn't until I spotted the entangled sea gull that I realized just how bad the plastic problem was. On a cleanup day during Coastweeks, I met with volunteers, slipped on gloves, grabbed large garbage bags, and slopped through tidal mud flats. We saw much more trash than we could pick up. But in the years ahead, if we all pitch in, we will see less trash and more gulls will fly free.

1. This passage is mostly about _____.
  (A) ocean tides and currents
  (B) trash in the ocean and on the coasts
  (C) animals that live near the ocean
  (D) why people throw their trash in the ocean

2. The word <u>debris</u> in the passage means _____.
  (A) sand
  (B) seashells
  (C) trash
  (D) food

3. According to the passage, ships dump trash into the ocean because _____.
  (A) trash is too heavy to keep on board
  (B) people on the ships don't like animals in the ocean
  (C) it is cheaper and easier than bringing trash to land
  (D) they know that trash will sink to the bottom of the ocean

4. It is worse to throw away plastic than paper, wood, or food because plastic _____.
  (A) does not decay as easily
  (B) should be used to make six-pack holders
  (C) has a bad odor
  (D) is more expensive than paper or wood

5. The word <u>decompose</u> in the passage means _____.

    Ⓐ last

    Ⓑ throw away

    Ⓒ break down

    Ⓓ survive

6. According to this passage, plastics in the water are dangerous because _____.

    Ⓐ they damage outer layers of boats

    Ⓑ sea animals eat them or get trapped in them

    Ⓒ people trip over them on the beach

    Ⓓ they poison our supply of drinking water

7. The author wrote this passage to _____.

    Ⓐ puzzle

    Ⓑ entertain

    Ⓒ confuse

    Ⓓ inform

8. The author of the passage seems to want readers to _____.

    Ⓐ go on an ocean trip

    Ⓑ help solve the trash problem

    Ⓒ keep sea turtles as pets

    Ⓓ learn more about ocean tides

Class Summary of Placement Test Results

Student Name	Levels Administered	Total Vocabulary	Total Comprehension	Grand Total	Placement Level	Comments

Phonemic Awareness Inventory
Summary of Performance

Name _____   Examiner _____

Task	Student's Score		
	Date _____	Date _____	Date _____
1. Segmenting Phonemes in a Word	/8	/8	/8
2. Deleting Words and Syllables	/8	/8	/8
3. Deleting Phonemes	/8	/8	/8
4. Substituting Initial and Final Sounds	/8	/8	/8
Total Score	/32	/32	/32

Performance Level:
Below 26 Would benefit from
individualized intervention
instruction
27 – 32 No or minimal additional
instruction required

Comments:

_____
_____
_____
_____
_____
_____
_____
_____
_____
_____
_____
_____

Phonemic Awareness Inventory
Administering and Recording Form
Task 1: Segmenting Phonemes in a Word

Task: The child will listen to a word and then will produce each phoneme in the word separately.

Model: **I am going to say a word. Then I am going to say each sound in the word. Listen carefully for each sound. The word is *go*. The sounds in go are /g/-/o/.** Be sure to articulate each sound separately. Do not simply stretch out the word.

Sample: **Listen to this word. This time you tell me the sounds in the word. Listen carefully: *man*. What sounds do you hear in *man*?** (/m/-/a/-/n/) **You're correct. The sounds in the word man are /m/-/a/-/n/.**

Now listen to some more words. Tell me the sounds you hear in these words.

Name _____

Item	Correct Response	Student's Response Date _____
1. dog	/d/-/o/-/g/	
2. keep	/k/-/ee/-/p/	
3. no	/n/-/o/	
4. that	/th/-/a/-/t/	
5. me	/m/-/ee/	
6. do	/d/-/oo/	
7. race	/r/-/a/-/s/	
8. in	/i/-/n/	

Total Score: _____/8

Comments:

_____

_____

_____

_____

Phonemic Awareness Inventory
Administering and Recording Form

Task 2: Deleting Words and Syllables

Task: The child will listen to a word and then delete a syllable from the word to create a new word.

Model: **Listen to this word—downtown. If I take off "down," the new word would be "town."**

Sample: **Now you try one. Listen to this word—inside. If you take off "in," what would the new word be?** Pause for response. Repeat directions if necessary. **You're correct. The new word would be "side."**

           Listen to some more words and tell me what the new words would be.

Name _____

Item	Correct Response	Student's Response
		Date _____
1. forget (for)	get	
2. skateboard (skate)	board	
3. baseball (base)	ball	
4. seabed (sea)	bed	
5. uphill (hill)	up	
6. replay (re)	play	
7. quickly (ly)	quick	
8. capful (ful)	cap	

Total Score: _____/8

Comments:

_____
_____
_____
_____
_____
_____

© Harcourt

Phonemic Awareness Inventory
Administering and Recording Form

Task 3: Deleting Phonemes

Task: The child will listen to a word and then delete a phoneme from the word to create a new word.

Model: **Listen to this word—wink. If I take off the /w/ sound, the new word would be "ink."**

Sample: **Now you try one. Listen to this word—sold. If you take off the /s/ sound, what would the new word be?** Pause for response. Repeat directions if necessary. **You're correct. The new word would be "old."**

Listen to some more words and tell me what the new words would be.

Name _____

Item	Correct Response	Student's Response Date _____
1. rice /r/	ice	
2. meat /m/	eat	
3. bus /b/	us	
4. rake /r/	-ake (ache)	
5. rose /s/	row	
6. beet /t/	bee	
7. park /k/	par	
8. bake /k/	bay	

Total Score: _____/8

Comments:

_____

_____

_____

_____

_____

_____

Phonemic Awareness Inventory
Administering and Recording Form
Task 4: Substituting Initial and Final Sounds

Task: The child will listen to a word and then replace either the initial or final phoneme to create a new word.

Model: **I am going to say a word. I want you to take off the first sound of the word and put in a new sound. Let's try one. If I change the first sound in "let" to /m/, the new word is "met."**

Sometimes I'll ask you to take off the end sound and put in a new sound. If I change the last sound in "bin" to /t/, the new word would be "bit."

Sample: **Change the first sound in "pop" to /t/. What would the new word be? Yes, the new word would be "top."**

Now listen to some more words. Tell me the new words you would make.

Name _____

Item	Correct Response	Student's Response Date _____
Substituting Initial Sounds		
1. pit /s/	sit	
2. cup /p/	pup	
3. net /g/	get	
4. sack /b/	back	
Substituting Final Sounds		
5. bud /s/	bus	
6. sad /p/	sap	
7. pet /g/	peg	
8. mop /m/	mom	

Total Score: _____/8

Comments:

_____

_____

_____

Phonics Inventory
Performance Profile

Name _____   Date _____

Section	Number Correct (Circle One)	Comments
1. CVC Words	0 1 2 3 4 5 6 7 8 9 10	
2. Consonant Blends	0 1 2 3 4 5 6 7 8 9 10	
3. Consonant Digraphs	0 1 2 3 4 5 6 7 8 9 10	
4. Long Vowels	0 1 2 3 4 5 6 7 8 9 10	
5. Vowels: Digraphs and Diphthongs/R-Controlled	0 1 2 3 4 5 6 7 8 9 10	
6. Multisyllabic Words	0 1 2 3 4 5 6 7 8 9 10	
Total Score		

Strengths: _____

_____

_____

_____

_____

Weaknesses: _____

_____

_____

_____

_____

Instructional Priorities: _____

_____

_____

_____

Phonics Inventory
Recording Form

CVC Words	Consonant Blends	Consonant Digraphs
Response	**Response**	**Response**
1. bem _____	1. clup _____	1. shan _____
2. sab _____	2. drat _____	2. chas _____
3. nid _____	3. flem _____	3. thib _____
4. kon _____	4. stim _____	4. whem _____
5. fip _____	5. grud _____	5. phat _____
6. jeg _____	6. nast _____	6. fong _____
7. lob _____	7. lipt _____	7. rath _____
8. tat _____	8. mesk _____	8. seck _____
9. vud _____	9. reft _____	9. resh _____
10. gen _____	10. pund _____	10. fitch _____
Score _____	**Score** _____	**Score** _____

CVCe Words	Vowels: Digraphs Dipthongs/R-Control	Multisyllabic Words
Response	**Response**	**Response**
1. nobe _____	1. neap _____	1. dabbet (dab-bet) _____
2. rafe _____	2. doil _____	2. pelrim (pel-rim) _____
3. tife _____	3. sook _____	3. ziptod (zip-tod) _____
4. dute _____	4. yaw _____	4. tabert (ta-bert) _____
5. lope _____	5. bir _____	5. jusold (ju-sold) _____
6. bame _____	6. zart _____	6. fokay (fo-kay) _____
7. kote _____	7. zowl _____	7. bicturing (bic-tur-ing) _____
8. nate _____	8. noy _____	8. sackbility (sack-bil-i-ty) _____
9. faine _____	9. tout _____	9. canberize (can-ber-ize) _____
10. breeme _____	10. gooze _____	10. trofounds (tro-founds) _____
Score _____	**Score** _____	**Score** _____

bem

sab

nid

kon

fip

jeg

lob

tat

vud

gen

clup

drat

flem

stim

grud

nast

lipt

mesk

reft

pund

shan

chas

thib

whem

phat

fong

rath

seck

resh

fitch

nobe

rafe

tife

dute

lope

bame

kote

nate

faine

breeme

neap

doil

sook

yaw

bir

zart

zowl

noy

tout

gooze

dabbet

pelrim

ziptod

tabert

jusold

fokay

bicturing

sackbility

canberize

trofounds

Multisyllabic Words